LEAN AND GREEN AIR FRYER COOKBOOK

Easy and Healthy Recipes to Lose Weight and Get Back in Shape. Boost your Metabolism and Save Money while Enjoying the Best Lean and Green Meals

Theresa Bowerman

Table of Contents

Chapter 1: What Is Air Frying?

With air frying, you can enjoy a variety of foods without adding any more oil than what your recipe calls for.

Air frying is when food cooks as the result of hot air being blown over it in a convection oven (or sometimes, in an open dryer). By using heated circulating air instead of cooking oil, less fat and fewer calories are added to your foods! The process happens much faster than baking at 400°F so it's also energy-efficient.

Air frying is a healthy alternative to deep-frying and it's a lot easier than most people think. The process is similar to baking, but the food cooks in less time. No more worries about splattering grease across your walls and ceiling!

Pros and Cons of Air Fryer

An air fryer is a kitchen appliance that typically generates dry, indirect heat to cook food through convection. There are two ways an air fryer can cook, with or without oil. An air fryer without oil does not require much less time to preheat and cook food than one that is cooking with oil. If you plan to be using your air fryer as a substitute for deep fat frying, chances are you will be using it with heated oil.

Pros

- You can cook healthy food in an air fryer that has a low-fat content.

- It will eliminate the need for additional oil, especially if you're frying lean and low-fat foods. Thus, it saves money and also helps reduce our carbon footprint.
- For those who are looking to make healthier meals at home without much hassle and with less time required to prepare them, this is a great alternative as it will save time getting your stuff done and will cut on energy consumption as well as produce less waste.

Cons

- It can be dangerous due to the hot surface temperature.
- The food will be cooked differently than you would expect due to the extra time required for cooking typical foods in oil before cooking in an air fryer.
- Purchasing an air fryer can be costly.
- If you are not careful enough, there is a possibility of fire, which could result in serious damage to your home.

Benefits of an Air Fryer

An air fryer is an appliance that uses the hot air circulating at high speed to cook your food. The cooking process uses 80% less oil than a conventional deep fryer, and it can be easier on the electrical bill because you will typically use less energy with an air fryer than a traditional oven or stovetop.

With this appliance popping up more and more in kitchens these days, it is important to know what it does and how it can provide some added convenience for your everyday cooking routine.

Features To Consider

Timer: An air fryer with a timer is a major convenience in that it reduces unnecessary oil usage as food can cook and be served at pre-set intervals. The timer also allows you to freeze your food without having to defrost or reheat it before serving.

Temperature Control: Used for both cooking and freezing, an air fryer with controls gives you the ability to change the temperature of the device while cooking or freezing. This is a huge convenience when you have a variety of foods that may not cooperate when cooked in one setting, such as raw meats (meats are often less tender when cooked at high temperatures).

Temperature Adjustment: Foods should never be frozen at temperatures higher than the manufacturer recommends. However, this is possible with air fryers that have adjustable temperature controls.

Cooking Basket: Although most people use their air fryer to cook single servings, some air fryers come with a cooking basket that permits frying foods in bulk. Just remove the basket and leftovers can be reheated or frozen for later use.

How It Works

The air fryer works by circulating hot air to cook the food. The circulating hot air creates a convection oven-like atmosphere that cooks the food.

The oil is not needed because the hot circulating atmosphere creates steam which prevents sticking and allows for crispier foods without using oil.

(Note: depending on what you are frying, your results may vary. Oily foods may not be as crispy when using air frying, but they will still be healthier than if you fry them in oil).

Chapter 2: Air Fryer Breakfast Recipes

Lean and Green Breakfast Cups

Preparation Time: 15 minutes

Cooking Time: 8 minutes

Servings: 4

Ingredients:

- 5 organic eggs
- 1organic egg white
- 2 green chilies, chopped
- 3 green onions, chopped
- 10 pieces of Canadian bacon, chopped
- 1 cup spinach, torn
- Salt and black pepper, to taste

Directions:

1. Preheat the Air fryer at 400°F for 10 minutes.
2. Take a bowl and whisk the eggs in it, then add egg white and whisk well.
3. Now add the green chilies, onions, chopped spinach and season it with salt and black pepper.

4. Grease ramekins with oil spray and add the bacon at the bottom.
5. Pour each ramekin with the egg mixture.
6. Place the ramekins inside the Air fryer and close the lid.
7. Bake it for 8 minutes at 375°F.
8. Once egg muffins are firm, serve them and enjoy.

Serving Suggestion: Serve it with toast

Variation Tip: Use kale instead of spinach

Nutrition:

- Calories: 312
- Fat: 15.5g
- Sodium: 210mg
- Carbs: 4g
- Fiber: 0.5g
- Sugar: 0.8g
- Protein: 37.7g

Zucchini Egg Muffins

Preparation Time: 15 minutes

Cooking Time: 22 minutes

Servings: 4

Ingredients:

- 4 cups grated fresh zucchinis, grated
- 1 tsp. olive oil
- 2 eggs, whisked
- ½ cup low-fat cheese
- 1/3 cup almond flour
- Salt and black pepper, to taste
- 1/3 tsp. garlic powder
- ¼ tsp. cumin, powder
- Oil spray, for greasing

Directions:

1. Soak the grated zucchini in salted water for 10 minutes, then drain and squeeze to take out the excess liquid.
2. Preheat the air fryer by selecting AIR FRY mode for 5 minutes at 350°F.
3. Select START/PAUSE to begin the preheating process.
4. Once preheating is done, press START/PAUSE.
5. Grease the ramekins with oil spray.
6. Set them aside for further use.

7. Heat olive oil in a skillet and cooked zucchinis for about 2 minutes
8. Then add garlic powder, salt, pepper, cumin in the skillet and cook for a minute.
9. Afterward, transfer it to a plate and let it get cool
10. Whisk an egg into a small bowl.
11. Add in the zucchini mixture
12. Whisk it well and then add the cheese and almond flour.
13. Divide this mixture between the greased ramekins.
14. Place the ramekins in the air fryer basket and air fry at 350F for 15 minutes.
15. Once done, serve it.

Serving Suggestion: Serve it with coffee

Variation Tip: You can skip almond flour if wanted

Nutrition:

- Calories: 133
- Fat: 9.5g
- Sodium: 131mg
- Carbs: 4.9g
- Fiber: 1.5g
- Sugar: 2.3g
- Protein: 8.2g

Lean and Green Cloud Bread

Preparation Time: 15 minutes

Cooking Time: 6 minutes

Servings: 2

Ingredients:

- 1/16 tsp. Cream of tartar
- 3 eggs separated
- ½ cup Greek yogurt, fat-free
- 2 tbsps. Stevia, or less

Directions:

1. Preheat the air fryer by selecting AIR FRY mode for 5 minutes at 300°F.
2. Put the whisking appliance in the refrigerator for 1 hour before starting the process.
3. Take a whisking bowl and add egg whites to it.
4. Add egg yolk to a separate bowl and add Greek yogurt and stevia.
5. Add cream of tartar to egg whites and start mixer to mix it until peaks form on top.
6. Do not over-stir.
7. Then add the egg yolk mixture to the egg whites and stir well.
8. Take a cake pan and place parchment paper on it.

9. Put this egg mixture in the cake pan and put it in the air fryer basket
10. Cook at air fry mode at 370°F for 6 minutes.
11. Once done, serve it.

Serving Suggestion: Serve it with tea.

Variation Tip: None

Nutrition:

- Calories: 32
- Fat: 0.5g
- Sodium: 33mg
- Carbs: 1.2g
- Fiber: 0g
- Sugar: 1.2g
- Protein: 5.2g

Air Fryer Egg Bite Cups

Preparation Time: 12 minutes

Cooking Time: 13 minutes

Servings: 6

Ingredients:

- 6 large eggs
- 2 tbsps. almond milk
- Salt and pepper to taste
- ¼ cup green peppers, chopped
- ¼ cup onions, chopped
- ¼ cup spinach, chopped
- ½ cup almond and cashew cream
- 3 slices crumbled bacon

Directions:

1. Take a mixing bowl and whisk eggs in it.
2. Then, the remaining listed ingredients 1 by 1, excluding crumbled bacon.
3. Keep whisking the ingredients for fine incorporation.
4. Place the silicone molds in the air fryer and pour in the egg mixture.
5. Top it with crumbled bacon.
6. Air fry it for 13-15 minutes at 310°F.

7. Insert the toothpick at the center of the cup, when it comes out clean, the eggs are done, serve and enjoy.

Serving Suggestion: Serve it with ketchup

Variation Tip: Use coconut milk instead of almond milk

Nutrition:

- Calories: 431
- Fat: 32.3g
- Sodium: 1540mg
- Carbs: 2.4g
- Fiber: 0.3g
- Sugar: 0.9g
- Protein: 30g

Baked Eggs for Breakfast

Preparation Time: 12 minutes

Cooking Time: 15 minutes

Servings: 4

Ingredients:

- 5 oz. Ham, sliced into pieces
- 2 cups baby spinach
- 4 organic eggs, refrigerated
- 2 tbsps. Almond milk
- ½ tsp. Olive oil
- Salt and pepper, to taste
- Oil spray, for greasing

Directions:

1. Preheat the air fryer to 300°F.
2. Now, grease 4 ramekins and set them aside.
3. Heat olive oil in a pan and sauté the baby spinach for 2 minutes.
4. Divide this cooked spinach between 4 ramekins.
5. Divide the ham between 4 ramekins.
6. Whisk the egg along with the milk, salt, and pepper.
7. Pour the egg in ramekins; remember not to fill it to the top.
8. Select the Bake function and bake it for about 15 minutes in the air fryer.

9. Serve and enjoy.

Serving Suggestion: Serve it with tea

Variation Tip: Use coconut milk instead of almond milk

Nutrition:

- Calories: 164
- Fat: 9.9g
- Sodium: 605mg
- Carbs: 7.1g
- Fiber: 3.1g
- Sugar: 0.6g
- Protein: 12.6g

Lean and Green Soufflé

Preparation Time: 10 minutes

Cooking Time: 10 minutes

Servings: 6

Ingredients:

- 6 organic eggs
- 6 tbsps. Cashew and almond cream
- Salt and black pepper, to taste
- 1 cup parsley, chopped

Directions:

1. Take a bowl and whisk the eggs in it along with parsley, cashew, and almond cream, and season it with salt and black pepper.
2. Grease the soufflé cup with oil spray.
3. Fill the soufflé cups halfway with the egg mixture.
4. Air fry it in the air fryer for 10 minutes at 375°F.
5. Serve and enjoy.

Serving Suggestion: Serve it with coffee.

Variation Tip: Use coconut cream instead of cashew and almond cream.

Nutrition:

- Calories: 122

- Fat: 8.2g
- Sodium: 116mg
- Carbs: 3g
- Fiber: 0.5g
- Sugar: 0.6g
- Protein: 8.8g

Frittata

Preparation Time: 15 minutes

Cooking Time: 20 minutes

Servings: 4

Ingredients:

- ¼ Pound breakfast sausage
- 4 eggs, beaten
- ½ cup cheddar cheese, shredded
- 2 tbsps. Green bell pepper, diced
- 1 green onion, chopped
- Cooking spray, for coating

Directions:

1. Combine sausage, eggs, cheese, bell pepper, and onions in a bowl and mix to combine.
2. Preheat the air fryer to 360°F.
3. Spray a nonstick 6-cake pan with cooking spray.
4. Place the egg mixture in the prepared cake pan.
5. Cook in the air fryer until the frittata is done, for about 18 to 20 minutes.

Serving Suggestion: Serve it with ketchup

Variation Tip: Use parmesan cheese that is low fat

Nutrition:

- Calories: 237
- Fat: 17.4g
- Sodium: 384mg
- Carbs: 5.3g
- Fiber: 0.9g
- Sugar: 3.5g
- Protein: 15.2g

Lean and Green Quiche

Preparation Time: 15 minutes

Cooking Time: 20 minutes

Servings: 4

Ingredients:

- 1 cup thinly sliced mushrooms
- 1 red bell pepper, chopped
- 2 cups eggs, whisked
- 4 oz. reduced-fat mozzarella
- 2 cups baby spinach
- ½ tsp. black pepper
- 1 tsp. garlic powder
- 1 tsp. olive oil

Directions:

1. Preheat the air fry to 350°F.
2. Meanwhile, the air fryer is preheating, in a skillet sauté the mushroom in olive oil and added bell pepper.
3. Sauté it for 2 minutes and then transfer it to a pan.
4. Allow it to cool.
5. In a separate large bowl, whisk the egg, milk, spinach, garlic powder, and pepper.
6. Mix in the sautéed mushrooms and red pepper mixture.
7. Take a pie plate and grease it with oil.

8. Then, pour in the mixture.

9. Add shredded cheese on top.

10. Bake the quiche for 20 minutes or more, until set.

Serving Suggestion: Serve it with coffee

Variation Tip: Use coconut oil instead of olive oil

Nutrition:

- Calories: 177
- Fat: 7.5g
- Sodium: 477mg
- Carbs: 6g
- Fiber: 1.1g
- Sugar: 2.8g
- Protein: 236g

Radish Hash Browns

Preparation Time: 10 minutes

Cooking Time: 13 minutes

Servings: 4

Ingredients:

- 1 lb. Radishes, washed and cut off roots
- 1 tbsps. Olive oil
- ½ tsp paprika
- ½ tsp onion powder
- ½ tsp garlic powder
- 1 medium onion
- ¼ tsp pepper
- ¾ tsp sea salt

Directions:

1. Slice the onion and radishes using a mandolin slicer.
2. Add sliced onion and radishes to a large mixing bowl and toss with olive oil.
3. Transfer the onion and radish slices in the air fryer basket and cook at 360°F for 8 minutes. Shake basket twice.
4. Return the onion and radish slices in a mixing bowl and toss with seasonings.

5. Again, cook the onion and radish slices in the air fryer basket for 5 minutes at 400°F. Shake basket halfway through.
6. Serve it and enjoy.

Nutrition:

- Calories: 62
- Fat: 3.7g
- Carbohydrates: 7.1g
- Sugar: 3.5g
- Protein: 1.2g
- Cholesterol: 0mg

Vegetable Egg Cups

Preparation Time: 10 minutes

Cooking Time: 20 minutes

Servings: 4

Ingredients:

- 4 eggs
- 1 tbsp. cilantro, chopped
- 4 tbsps. Half and half
- 1 cup cheddar cheese, shredded
- 1 cup vegetables, diced
- Pepper
- Salt

Directions:

1. Spray 4 ramekins with cooking spray and set them aside.
2. In a mixing bowl, whisk the eggs with the cilantro, half and half, vegetables, ½ cup cheese, pepper, and salt.
3. Pour the egg mixture into the 4 ramekins.
4. Place the ramekins in the air fryer basket and cook at 300°F for 12 minutes.
5. Top with the remaining ½ cup cheese and cook for 2 minutes more at 400°F.
6. Serve it and enjoy.

Nutrition:

- Calories: 194
- Fat: 11.5g
- Carbohydrates: 6g
- Sugar: 0.5g
- Protein: 13g
- Cholesterol: 190mg

Spinach Frittata

Preparation Time: 5 minutes

Cooking Time: 8 minutes

Servings: 1

Ingredients:

- 3 eggs
- 1 cup spinach, chopped
- 1 small onion, minced
- 2 tbsps. mozzarella cheese, grated
- Pepper
- Salt

Directions:

1. Preheat the air fryer to 350°F.
2. Spray the air fryer pan with cooking spray.
3. In a bowl, whisk the eggs with the remaining ingredients until well combined.
4. Pour the egg mixture into the prepared pan and place the pan in the air fryer basket.
5. Cook the frittata for 8 minutes or until set.
6. Serve it and enjoy.

Nutrition:

- Calories: 384
- Fat: 23.3g

- Carbohydrates: 10.7g
- Sugar: 4.1g
- Protein: 34.3g
- Cholesterol: 521mg

Omelette Frittata

Preparation Time: 10 minutes

Cooking Time: 6 minutes

Servings: 2

Ingredients:

- 3 eggs, lightly beaten
- 2 tbsps. cheddar cheese, shredded
- 2 tbsps. heavy cream
- 2 mushrooms, sliced
- ¼ small onion, chopped
- ¼ bell pepper, diced
- Pepper
- Salt

Directions:

1. In a bowl, whisk the eggs with cream, vegetables, pepper, and salt.
2. Preheat the air fryer to 400°F.
3. Pour the egg mixture into the air fryer pan. Place the pan in the air fryer basket and cook for 5 minutes.
4. Add shredded cheese on top of the frittata and cook it for 1 minute more.
5. Serve it and enjoy.

Nutrition:

- Calories: 160
- Fat: 10g
- Carbohydrates: 4g
- Sugar: 2g
- Protein: 12g
- Cholesterol: 255mg

Cheese Soufflés

Preparation Time: 10 minutes

Cooking Time: 6 minutes

Servings: 8

Ingredients:

- 6 large eggs, separated
- ¾ cup heavy cream
- ¼ tsp cayenne pepper
- ½ tsp xanthan gum
- ½ tsp pepper
- ¼ tsp cream of tartar
- 2 tbsps. chives, chopped
- 2 cups cheddar cheese, shredded
- 1 tsp salt
- Almond flour

Directions:

1. Preheat the air fryer to 325 F.
2. Spray 8 ramekins with cooking spray. Set them aside.
3. In a bowl, whisk together the almond flour, cayenne pepper, pepper, salt, and xanthan gum.
4. Slowly, add the heavy cream and mix to combine.
5. Whisk in the egg yolks, chives, and cheese until well combined.

6. In a large bowl, add the egg whites and the cream of tartar and beat until stiff peaks form.
7. Fold the egg white mixture into the almond flour mixture until combined.
8. Pour the mixture into the prepared ramekins. Divide the ramekins into batches.
9. Place the first batch of ramekins into the air fryer basket.
10. Cook the soufflé for 20 minutes.
11. Serve it and enjoy.

Nutrition:

- Calories: 210
- Fat: 16g
- Carbohydrates: 1g
- Sugar: 0.5g
- Protein: 12g
- Cholesterol: 185mg

Simple Egg Soufflé

Preparation Time: 5 minutes

Cooking Time: 8 minutes

Servings: 2

Ingredients:

- 2 eggs
- ¼ tsp chili pepper
- 2 tbsps. heavy cream
- ¼ tsp pepper
- 1 tbsps. parsley, chopped
- Salt

Directions:

1. In a bowl, whisk eggs with the remaining gradients.
2. Spray 2 ramekins with cooking spray.
3. Pour the egg mixture into the prepared ramekins and place them into the air fryer basket.
4. Cook the soufflé at 390°F for 8 minutes.
5. Serve it and enjoy.

Nutrition:

- Calories: 116
- Fat: 10g
- Carbohydrates: 1.1g
- Sugar: 0.4g

- Protein: 6g
- Cholesterol: 184mg

Vegetable Egg Soufflé

Preparation Time: 10 minutes

Cooking Time: 20 minutes

Servings: 4

Ingredients:

- 4 large eggs
- 1 tsp onion powder
- 1 tsp garlic powder
- 1 tsp red pepper, crushed
- ½ cup broccoli florets, chopped
- ½ cup mushrooms, chopped

Directions:

1. Spray 4 ramekins with cooking spray and set aside.
2. In a bowl, whisk the eggs with onion powder, garlic powder, and red pepper.
3. Add the mushrooms and broccoli and stir well.
4. Pour the egg mixture into the prepared ramekins and place them into the air fryer basket.
5. Cook at 350°F for 15 minutes. Make sure the soufflé is cooked, if it's not cooked, then cook it for 5 more minutes.
6. Serve it and enjoy.

Nutrition:

- Calories: 91

- Fat: 5.1g
- Carbohydrates: 4.7g
- Sugar: 2.6g
- Protein: 7.4g
- Cholesterol: 186mg

Chapter 3: Air Fryer Lunch Recipes

Easy Rosemary Lamb Chops

Preparation Time: 10 minutes

Cooking Time: 6 minutes

Servings: 4

Ingredients:

- 4 lamb chops
- 2 tbsps. dried rosemary
- ¼ cup fresh lemon juice
- Pepper
- Salt

Directions:

1. In a small bowl, mix the lemon juice, rosemary, pepper, and salt.
2. Brush the lemon juice-rosemary mixture over the lamb chops.
3. Place the lamb chops on the air fryer oven tray and air fry setting at 400°F for 3 minutes.
4. Turn the lamb chops to the other side and cook them for 3 minutes more.
5. Serve it and enjoy.

Nutrition:

- Calories: 267
- Fat: 21.7g
- Carbohydrates: 1.4g
- Sugar: 0.3g
- Protein: 16.9g
- Cholesterol: 0mg

Juicy Steak Bites

Preparation Time: 10 minutes

Cooking Time: 9 minutes

Servings: 4

Ingredients:

- 1 lb. sirloin steak, cut into bite-size pieces
- 1 tbsps. steak seasoning
- 1 tbsps. olive oil
- Pepper
- Salt

Directions:

1. Preheat the air fryer oven to 390°F.
2. Add the steak pieces into the large mixing bowl. Add steak seasoning, oil, pepper, and salt over the steak pieces and toss until well coated.
3. Transfer the steak pieces to the air fryer pan and air fry for 5 minutes.
4. Turn the steak pieces to the other side and cook them for 4 minutes more. Serve them and enjoy.

Nutrition:

- Calories: 241
- Fat: 10.6g
- Carbohydrates: 0g

- Sugar: 0g
- Protein: 34.4g
- Cholesterol: 101mg

Greek Lamb Chops

Preparation Time: 10 minutes

Cooking Time: 10 minutes

Servings: 4

Ingredients:

- 2 lbs. lamb chops
- 2 tsp garlic, minced
- 1½ tsp dried oregano
- ¼ cup fresh lemon juice
- ¼ cup olive oil
- ½ tsp pepper
- 1 tsp salt

Directions:

1. Add the lamb chops to a mixing bowl. Add the remaining ingredients over the lamb chops and coat well.
2. Arrange the lamb chops on the air fryer oven tray and cook at 400°F for 5 minutes.
3. Turn the lamb chops and cook it for 5 minutes more.
4. Serve it and enjoy.

Nutrition:

- Calories: 538
- Fat: 29.4g
- Carbohydrates: 1.3g

- Sugar: 0.4g
- Protein: 64g
- Cholesterol: 204mg

Easy Beef Roast

Preparation Time: 10 minutes

Cooking Time: 45 minutes

Servings: 6

Ingredients:

- 2½ lbs. beef roast
- 2 tbsps. Italian seasoning

Directions:

1. Arrange the roast on the rotisserie spite.
2. Rub the roast with Italian seasoning, then insert it into the air fryer oven.
3. Air fry at 350°F for 45 minutes or until the roast's internal temperature reaches 145 F.
4. Slice and serve it.

Nutrition:

- Calories: 365
- Fat: 13.2g
- Carbohydrates: 0.5g
- Sugar: 0.4g
- Protein: 57.4g
- Cholesterol: 172mg

Buttermilk Marinated Chicken

Preparation Time: 10 minutes

Cooking Time: 25 minutes

Servings: 6

Ingredients:

- 3 lb. whole chicken
- 1 tbsp. salt
- 1 pint buttermilk

Directions:

1. Place the whole chicken in a large bowl and drizzle salt on top.
2. Pour the buttermilk over it and leave the chicken soaked overnight.
3. Cover the chicken bowl and refrigerate overnight.
4. Remove the chicken and fix it on the rotisserie rod in the air fryer.
5. Air Roast and set the cooking time to 25 minutes. Set the temperature at 370°F.
6. Close its lid and allow the chicken to roast.
7. Serve it warm.

Nutrition:

- Calories: 284
- Fat: 7.9g

- Carbs: 46g
- Fiber: 3.6g
- Sugar: 5.5g
- Protein: 17.9g

Teriyaki Glazed Chicken Bake

Preparation Time: 10 minutes

Cooking Time: 30 minutes

Servings: 2

Ingredients:

- 2 tbsps. cider vinegar
- 4 skinless chicken thighs
- 1½ tsps. cornstarch
- 1½ tsps. cold water
- ½ clove garlic, minced
- ¼ cup white sugar
- ¼ cup soy sauce
- ¼ tsp. ground ginger
- 1/8 tsp. ground black pepper

Directions:

1. Lightly grease the baking pan of the air fryer with cooking spray. Add all the ingredients and toss well to coat. Spread the chicken in a single layer on the bottom of the pan.
2. For 15 minutes, cook at 390°F.
3. Turnover the chicken while brushing and covering well with the sauce.
4. Cook it for 15 minutes at 330°F.
5. Serve it and enjoy.

Nutrition:

- Calories: 267
- Carbs: 19.9g
- Protein: 24.7g
- Fat: 9.8g

Sriracha-Ginger Chicken

Preparation Time: 10 minutes

Cooking Time: 35 minutes

Servings: 3

Ingredients:

- ¼ cup fish sauce
- ¼ cup Sriracha
- ½ cup light brown sugar
- ½ cup rice vinegar
- 1½ pounds chicken breasts, pounded
- 1/3 cup hot chili paste
- 2 tsps. grated and peeled ginger

Directions:

1. Place all the ingredients in a Ziploc bag and allow to marinate for at least 2 hours in the fridge.
2. Preheat the air fryer to 390°F.
3. Place the grill pan accessory in the air fryer.
4. Grill the chicken for 25 minutes.
5. Flip the chicken every 10 minutes for even grilling.
6. Meanwhile, pour the marinade into a saucepan and heat it over medium flame until the sauce thickens.
7. Before serving the chicken, brush with the Sriracha glaze.

Nutrition:

- Calories: 415
- Carbs: 5.4g
- Protein: 49.3g
- Fat: 21.8g

Naked Cheese, Chicken Stuffing 'n Green Beans

Preparation Time: 10 minutes

Cooking Time: 20 minutes

Servings: 3

Ingredients:

- 1 cup cooked, cubed chicken breast meat
- ½ (10.75 oz.) can condensed cream of chicken soup
- ½ (14.5 oz.) can green beans, drained
- ½ cup shredded Cheddar cheese
- 6 oz. unseasoned dry bread stuffing mix
- Salt and pepper to taste

Directions:

1. Mix well the pepper, salt, soup, and chicken in a medium bowl.
2. Make the stuffing according to package Directions for Cooking.
3. Lightly grease the baking pan of the air fryer with cooking spray. Evenly spread the chicken mixture on the bottom of the pan. Top evenly with stuffing. Sprinkle cheese on top.
4. Cover the pan with foil.
5. For 15 minutes, cook it at 390°F.

6. Remove the foil and cook for 5 minutes at 390°F until the tops are lightly browned.
7. Serve it and enjoy.

Nutrition:

- Calories: 418
- Carbs: 48.8g
- Protein: 27.1g
- Fat: 12.7g

Grilled Chicken Pesto

Preparation Time: 10 minutes

Cooking Time: 30 minutes

Servings: 8

Ingredients:

- 1¾ cup commercial pesto
- 8 chicken thighs
- Salt and pepper to taste

Directions:

1. Place all the ingredients in the Ziploc bag and allow to marinate in the fridge for at least 2 hours.
2. Preheat the air fryer to 390°F.
3. Place the grill pan accessory in the air fryer.
4. Grill the chicken for at least 30 minutes.
5. Make sure to flip the chicken every 10 minutes for even grilling.

Nutrition:

- Calories: 477
- Carbs: 3.8g
- Protein: 32.6g
- Fat: 36.8g

Crusted Cauliflower

Preparation Time: 5 minutes

Cooking Time: 15 minutes

Total Time: 20 minutes

Servings: 04

Ingredients:

- 1 cauliflower head, diced into chunks
- ½ unsweetened non-dairy milk
- 6 tbsps. Vegan mayo soy-free
- ¼ cup chickpea flour
- ¾ cup almond meal
- ¼ cup cornmeal
- 1 tsp. Onion powder
- 1 tsp. Garlic powder
- 1 tsp. Sea salt
- ½ tsp. Paprika
- Pinch of black pepper
- Cooking oil spray

Directions:

1. Preheat air fryer to 400°F.
2. Add and mix all the ingredients in a bowl, except the cauliflower.
3. Add the cauliflower chunks and toss well to coat.

4. Place the chunks in the air fryer basket.
5. Spray the cauliflower with cooking oil.
6. Cook for 15 minutes until cauliflower turns golden brown.
7. Garnish with parsley.
8. Serve it warm with your favorite sauce.

Nutrition:

- Calories: 248
- Total Fat: 15.7g
- Saturated Fat: 2.7g
- Cholesterol: 75mg
- Sodium: 94mg
- Total Carbs: 0.4g
- Fiber: 0g
- Sugar: 0g
- Protein: 24.9g

Sunday Fish with Sticky Sauce

Preparation Time: 20 minutes

Cooking Time: 11 minutes

Servings: 2

Ingredients:

- 2 Pollack fillets
- Salt and black pepper, to taste
- 1 tbsp. olive oil
- 1 cup chicken broth
- 2 tbsps. light soy sauce
- 1 tbsp. brown sugar
- 2 tbsps. butter, melted
- 1 tsp. fresh ginger, minced
- 1 tsp. fresh garlic, minced
- 2 corn tortillas

Directions:

1. Pat dry the Pollack fillets and season them with salt and black pepper; drizzle the sesame oil all over the fish fillets.
2. Preheat the Air Fryer to 380°F and cook your fish for 11 minutes. Slice into bite-sized pieces.
3. Meanwhile, prepare the sauce. Add the broth to a large saucepan and bring it to a boil. Add the soy sauce, sugar,

butter, ginger, and garlic. Reduce the heat to simmer and cook until it is reduced slightly.

4. Add the fish pieces to the warm sauce. Serve it on corn tortillas and enjoy!

Nutrition:

- Calories: 573
- Fat: 38.3g
- Carbs: 31.5g
- Protein: 26.2g
- Sugar: 7g

Tasty Air Fried Cod

Preparation Time: 10 minutes

Cooking Time: 12 minutes

Servings: 4

Ingredients:

- 7 oz. 2 cod fish
- Sesame oil
- Salt and black pepper
- 1 cup water
- 1 tsp. dark soy sauce
- 4 tbsp. light soy sauce
- 1 tbsp. sugar
- 3 tbsp. olive oil
- 4 ginger slices
- 3 spring onions
- 2 tbsp. coriander

Directions:

1. Season the fish with pepper, salt, sprinkle sesame oil, rub well and set it for 10 minutes.
2. Add the fish to the air fryer. Cook it at 356°F for 12 minutes.

3. Heat a pot with the water over medium heat. Add the sugar and light and dark soy sauce. Allow simmering. Take off the heat.
4. Heat the pan with olive oil over medium heat. Add the green onions and ginger. Cook for a few minutes. Take off the heat.
5. Divide the fish between plates. Top it with ginger and green onions. Drizzle the soy sauce mix. Sprinkle coriander and serve it.

Nutrition:

- Calories: 524
- Total Fat: 27.5g
- Sodium: 252mg
- Total Carbs: 56.2g
- Fiber: 2.3g
- Sugar: 20.3g
- Protein: 26.6g

Delicious Catfish

Preparation Time: 10 minutes

Cooking Time: 20 minutes

Servings: 4

Ingredients:

- 4 catfish fillets
- Black pepper and Salt
- A pinch of sweet paprika
- 1 tbsp. parsley
- 1 tbsp. lemon juice
- 1 tbsp. olive oil

Directions:

1. Season the catfish fillets with salt, paprika, pepper, drizzle oil, rub well. Then put in the air fryer basket and cook them at 400°F for 20 minutes. Flip the fish after 10 minutes.
2. Share the fish on plates. Sprinkle parsley and drizzle some lemon juice over it, serve it.

Nutrition:

- Calories: 247
- Total Fat: 15.7g
- Sodium: 86mg
- Total Carbs: 0.2g
- Fiber: 0.1g

- Sugar: 0.1g
- Protein: 25g

Cod Fillets with Fennel and Grapes Salad

Preparation Time: 10 minutes

Cooking Time: 15 minutes

Servings: 2

Ingredients:

- 2 black cod fillets
- 1 tbsp. olive oil
- Black pepper and Salt
- 1 fennel bulb
- 1 cup grapes
- ½ cup pecans

Directions:

1. Sprinkle half of the oil over the fish fillets, season with pepper and salt, rub well, place the fillets in the air fryer basket. Then, cook them for 10 minutes at 400°F and put them on the plate.
2. Mix pecans with grapes, fennel, the rest of the oil, salt, and pepper, toss to coat in a bowl. Add to the pan that fits the air fryer. Cook at 400°F for 5 minutes.
3. Share the cod on plates, add the grapes and fennel mix on the side, then serve it.

Nutrition:

- Calories: 602
- Total Fat: 50.4g
- Sodium: 132mg
- Total Carbs: 21.4g
- Fiber: 7g
- Sugar: 8.5g
- Protein: 21.7g

Tabasco Shrimp

Preparation Time: 10 minutes

Cooking Time: 10 minutes

Servings: 4

Ingredients:

- 1 lb. shrimp
- 1 tbsp. red pepper flakes
- 2 tbsp. olive oil
- 1 tbsp. Tabasco sauce
- 2 tbsp. water
- 1 tbsp. oregano
- Black pepper and salt
- ½ tbsp. parsley
- ½ tbsp. smoked paprika

Directions:

1. Mix the oil with the water, pepper flakes, Tabasco sauce, oregano, parsley, pepper, salt, paprika, and shrimp and toss well to coat in a bowl
2. Place shrimp to the preheated air fryer at 370°F and cook for 10 minutes. Shake the fryer once.
3. Share the shrimp on plates, then serve them with a side salad.

Nutrition:

- Calories: 206
- Total Fat: 9.4g
- Sodium: 301mg
- Total Carbs: 3.7g
- Fiber: 1.2g
- Sugar: 0.3g
- Protein: 26.3g

Chapter 4: Air Fryer Dinner Recipes

Cheesy Potato Casserole the Amish Way

Preparation Time: 15 minutes

Cooking Time: 45 minutes

Servings: 6

Ingredients:

- 2 cups frozen shredded hash brown potatoes, thawed
- 5 medium eggs, lightly beaten
- 1 cup shredded Cheddar cheese
- ½-pound sliced bacon, diced
- ½ sweet onion, chopped
- ½ cup and 2 tbsps. shredded Swiss cheese
- ¾ cup small curd cottage cheese

Directions:

1. Lightly grease the baking pan of the air fryer with cooking spray.
2. For 10 minutes, cook at 330°F the onion and bacon. Discard excess fat.

3. Meanwhile, in a bowl, whisk well the Swiss cheese, cottage cheese, cheddar cheese, eggs, and potatoes. Pour into the pan of cooked bacon and mix it well.
4. Cook for another 25 minutes.
5. Let it stand in the air fryer for another 10 minutes.
6. Serve it and enjoy.

Nutrition:

- Calories Per Serving: 341
- Carbs: 12.1g
- Protein: 21.7g
- Fat: 22.8g

Cheesy Sausage and Grits Bake from Down South

Preparation Time: 10 minutes

Cooking Time: 30 minutes

Servings: 4

Ingredients:

- ½ cup uncooked grits
- ¼ pound ground pork sausage
- 1½ cups water
- 2 tbsps. butter, divided
- 2 tbsps. milk
- 3 eggs
- ¾ cup shredded Cheddar cheese, divided
- Salt and pepper to taste

Directions:

1. In a large saucepan, bring water to a boil. Stir in the grits and simmer until the liquid is absorbed around 5 minutes. Stir in ¼ cup of cheese and 1 tbsps. of butter. Mix well until thoroughly incorporated.
2. Lightly grease the baking pan of the air fryer with cooking spray. Add the pork sausage and for 5 minutes, cook at 360°F. Crumble the sausage and discard excess fat.
3. Transfer the grits into the pan of sausage.

4. In a bowl, whisk well the milk and eggs and pour them into the pan. Mix well.
5. Dot the top with butter and sprinkle cheese. Season with pepper and salt.
6. Cook until tops are browned, around 20 minutes.
7. Serve it and enjoy.

Nutrition:

- Calories Per Serving: 403
- Carbs: 16.8g
- Protein: 16.5g
- Fat: 29.9g

Easy Peasy Pizza

Preparation Time: 5 minutes

Cooking Time: 9 minutes

Servings: 1

Ingredients:

- Cooking oil spray (coconut, sunflower, or safflower)
- 1 flour tortilla, preferably sprouted or whole grain
- ¼ cup vegan pizza or marinara sauce
- 1/3 cup grated vegan mozzarella cheese or Cheesy Sauce
- Toppings of your choice

Directions:

1. Spray the air fryer basket with oil. Place the tortilla in the air fryer basket. If the tortilla is a little bigger than the base, no probs! Simply, fold the edges up a bit to form a semblance of a "crust."
2. Pour the sauce in the center and evenly distribute it around the tortilla "crust" (I like to use the back of a spoon for this purpose).
3. Sprinkle evenly with vegan cheese and add your toppings. Bake for 9 minutes or until nicely browned. Remove carefully, cut into 4 pieces, and enjoy.

Nutrition:

- Calories: 210
- Total Fat: 6g
- Saturated Fat: 1g
- Cholesterol: 0mg
- Sodium: 700mg
- Carbohydrates: 33g
- Fiber: 2g
- Protein: 5g

Pasta with Creamy Cauliflower Sauce

Preparation Time: 10 minutes

Cooking Time: 18 minutes

Servings: 4

Ingredients:

- 4 cups cauliflower florets
- Cooking oil spray (sunflower, safflower, or refined coconut)
- 1 medium onion, chopped
- 8 oz. Pasta, your choice (about 4 cups cooked; use gluten-free pasta if desired)
- Fresh chives or scallion tops, for garnish
- ½ cup raw cashew pieces (see ingredient tip)
- 1½ cups water
- 1 tbsp. Nutritional yeast
- 2 large garlic cloves, peeled
- 2 tbsps. Fresh lemon juice
- 1½ tsps. Sea salt
- ¼ tsp. Freshly ground black pepper

Directions:

1. Place the cauliflower in the air fryer basket, spritz the tops with oil spray, and roast for 8 minutes. Remove the air

fryer basket, stir and add the onion. Spritz with oil again and roast for another 10 minutes or until the cauliflower is browned and the onions are tender.

2. While the vegetables are roasting in the air fryer, cook the pasta according to the package directions and mince the chives or scallions. Set it aside.

3. In a blender jar, place the roasted cauliflower and onions along with the cashews, water, nutritional yeast, garlic, lemon, salt, and pepper. Blend well, until very smooth and creamy. Serve a generous portion of the sauce on top of the warm pasta and top with the minced chives or scallions. The sauce will be stored, refrigerated in an airtight container, for about a week.

Nutrition:

- Calories: 341
- Total Fat: 9g
- Saturated Fat: 1g
- Cholesterol: 0mg
- Sodium: 312mg
- Carbohydrates: 51g
- Fiber: 6g
- Protein: 14g

Lemony Lentils with "Fried" Onions

Preparation Time: 10 minutes

Cooking Time: 30 minutes

Servings: 4

Ingredients:

- 1 cup red lentils
- 4 cups water
- Cooking oil spray (coconut, sunflower, or safflower)
- 1 medium-size onion, peeled and cut into ¼-inch-thick rings
- Sea salt
- ½ cup kale stems removed, thinly sliced
- 3 large garlic cloves, pressed or minced
- 2 tbsps. fresh lemon juice
- 2 tsps. Nutrition yeast
- 1 tsp. sea salt
- 1 tsp. lemon zest (see Ingredient Tip)
- ¾ tsp. freshly ground black pepper

Directions:

1. In a medium-large pot, bring the lentils and water to a boil over medium-high heat. Reduce the heat to low and simmer, uncovered, for about 30 minutes (or until the

lentils have dissolved completely), making sure to stir every 5 minutes or so as they cook (so that the lentils don't stick to the bottom of the pot).

2. While the lentils are cooking, get the rest of your dish together. Spray the air fryer basket with oil and place the onion rings inside, separating them as much as possible. Spray them with the oil and sprinkle with a little salt. Fry for 5 minutes. Remove the air fryer basket, shake or stir, spray again with oil and fry for another 5 minutes (Note: You're aiming for all of the onion slices to be crisp and well browned, so if some of the pieces begin to do that, transfer them from the air fryer basket to a plate).

3. Remove the air fryer basket, spray the onions again with oil and fry for a final 5 minutes or until all the pieces are crisp and browned.

4. To finish the lentils: Add the kale to the hot lentils and stir very well, as the heat from the lentils will steam the thinly sliced greens. Stir in the garlic, lemon juice, nutritional yeast, salt, zest, and pepper. Stir very well and then distribute evenly in bowls. Top with the crisp onion rings and serve.

Nutrition:

- Calories: 220
- Total Fat: 1g
- Saturated Fat: 0g
- Cholesterol: 0mg
- Sodium: 477mg

- Carbohydrates: 39g
- Fiber: 16g
- Protein: 15g

Our Daily Bean

Preparation Time: 5 minutes

Cooking Time: 8 minutes

Servings: 2

Ingredients:

- 1 (15-oz.) can pinto beans, drained
- ¼ cup tomato sauce
- 2 tbsps. Nutritional yeast
- 2 large garlic cloves, pressed or minced
- ½ tsp. dried oregano
- ½ tsp. cumin
- ¼ tsp. sea salt
- ⅛ tsp. freshly ground black pepper
- Cooking oil spray (sunflower, safflower, or refined coconut)

Directions:

1. In a medium bowl, stir together the beans, tomato sauce, nutritional yeast, garlic, oregano, cumin, salt, and pepper until well combined.

2. Spray the 6-inch round, 2-inch-deep baking pan with oil and pour the bean mixture into it. Bake for 4 minutes. Remove, stir well and bake for another 4 minutes, or until the mixture has thickened and is heated through. It will

most likely form a little crust on top and be lightly browned in spots. Serve it hot. This will keep, refrigerated in an airtight container, for up to a week.

Nutrition:

- Calories: 284
- Total Fat: 4g
- Saturated Fat: 1g
- Cholesterol: 0mg
- Sodium: 807mg
- Carbohydrates: 47g
- Fiber: 16g
- Protein: 20g

Taco Salad with Creamy Lime Sauce

Preparation Time: 7 minutes

Cooking Time: 20 minutes

Servings: 3

Ingredients:

For The Sauce:

- 1 (12.3-oz.) package of silken-firm tofu
- ¼ cup plus 1 tbsp. fresh lime juice
- 1 tsp. Zest 1 large lime
- 1½ tbsps. coconut sugar
- 3 large garlic cloves, peeled
- 1 tsp. sea salt
- ½ tsp. ground chipotle powder

For The Salad:

- 6 cups romaine lettuce, chopped (1 large head)
- 1 (15-oz.) can vegan refried beans (or whole pinto or black beans if you prefer)
- 1 cup chopped red cabbage
- 2 medium tomatoes, chopped
- ½ cup chopped cilantro
- ¼ cup minced scallions

- A double batch of Garlic Lime Tortilla Chips

Directions:

To Make the Sauce:

1. Drain the tofu (pour off any liquid) and place it in a blender. Add the lime juice and zest, coconut sugar, garlic, salt, and chipotle powder. Blend until very smooth. Set aside.

To Make the Salad:

2. Distribute the lettuce equally into 3 big bowls.
3. In a small pan over medium heat, warm the beans, stirring often, until hot (this should take less than a minute). Place on top of the lettuce. Top the beans with cabbage, tomatoes, cilantro, and scallions. Drizzle generously with the Creamy Lime Sauce and serve with the double batch of air-fried chips. Enjoy immediately.

Nutrition:

- Calories: 422
- Total Fat: 7g
- Saturated Fat: 1g
- Cholesterol: 0mg
- Sodium: 1186mg
- Carbohydrates: 71g
- Fiber: 15g
- Protein: 22g

BBQ Jackfruit Nachos

Preparation Time: 30 minutes

Cooking Time: 20 minutes

Servings: 3

Ingredients:

- 1 (20-oz.) can jackfruit, drained
- 1/3 cup prepared vegan BBQ sauce
- ¼ cup of water
- 2 tbsps. tamari or shoyu
- 1 tbsp. fresh lemon juice
- 4 large garlic cloves, pressed or minced
- 1 tsp. onion granules
- ⅛ tsp. cayenne powder
- ⅛ tsp. liquid smoke
- Double batch Garlic Lime Tortilla Chips
- 2½ cups prepared Cheesy Sauce
- 3 medium-size tomatoes, chopped
- ¾ cup guacamole of your choice
- ¾ cup chopped cilantro
- ½ cup minced red onion
- 1 jalapeño, seeds removed and thinly sliced (optional)

Directions:

1. In a large skillet over high heat, place the jackfruit, BBQ sauce, water, tamari, lemon juice, garlic, onion granules, cayenne, and liquid smoke. Stir well and break up the jackfruit a bit with a spatula.
2. Once the mixture boils, reduce the heat to low. Continue to cook, stirring often (and breaking up the jackfruit as you stir), for about 20 minutes, or until all of the liquid has been absorbed. Remove from the heat and set it aside.
3. Assemble the nachos: Distribute the chips onto 3 plates, and then top evenly with the jackfruit mixture, warmed Cheesy Sauce, tomatoes, guacamole, cilantro, onion, and jalapeño (if using). Enjoy immediately, because soggy chips are tragic.

Nutrition:

- Calories: 661
- Total Fat: 15g
- Saturated Fat: 1g
- Cholesterol: 0mg
- Sodium: 1842mg
- Carbohydrates: 124g
- Fiber: 19g
- Protein: 22g

10-Minute Chimichanga

Preparation Time: 2 minutes

Cooking Time: 8 minutes

Servings: 1

Ingredients:

- 1 whole-grain tortilla
- ½ cup vegan refried beans
- ¼ cup grated vegan cheese (optional)
- Cooking oil spray (sunflower, safflower, or refined coconut)
- ½ cup fresh salsa (or Green Chili Sauce)
- 2 cups chopped romaine lettuce (about ½ head)
- Guacamole (optional)
- Chopped cilantro (optional)
- Cheesy Sauce (optional)

Directions:

1. Lay the tortilla on a flat surface and place the beans in the center. Top with the cheese if using. Wrap the bottom up over the filling and then fold in the sides. Then roll it all up to enclose the beans inside the tortilla (you're making an enclosed burrito here).
2. Spray the air fryer basket with oil, place the tortilla wrap inside the basket, seam-side down, and spray the top of the

chimichanga with oil. Fry for 5 minutes. Spray the top (and sides) again with oil, flip over and spray the other side with oil. Fry for an additional 2 or 3 minutes, until nicely browned and crisp.

3. Transfer to a plate. Top with salsa, lettuce, guacamole, cilantro and/or Cheesy Sauce if using. Serve it immediately.

Nutrition:

- Calories: 317
- Total Fat: 6g
- Saturated Fat: 2g
- Cholesterol: 0mg
- Sodium: 955mg
- Carbohydrates: 55g
- Fiber: 11g
- Protein: 13g

Mexican Stuffed Potatoes

Preparation Time: 15 minutes

Cooking Time: 40 minutes

Servings: 4

Ingredients:

- 4 large potatoes, any variety (I like Yukon Gold or russets for this dish; see Cooking Tip)
- Cooking oil spray (sunflower, safflower, or refined coconut)
- 1½ cups Cheesy Sauce
- 1 cup black or pinto beans (canned beans are fine; be sure to drain and rinse)
- 2 medium tomatoes, chopped
- 1 scallion, finely chopped
- 1/3 cup finely chopped cilantro
- 1 jalapeño, finely sliced or minced (optional)
- 1 avocado, diced (optional)

Directions:

1. Scrub the potatoes, prick with a fork and spray the outsides with oil. Place in the air fryer (leaving room in between so the air can circulate) and bake them for 30 minutes.
2. While the potatoes are cooking, prepare the Cheesy Sauce and additional items. Set them aside.

3. Check the potatoes at the 30-minute mark by poking a fork into them. If they're very tender, they're done. If not, continue to cook until a fork inserted proves them to be well-done (As potato sizes vary, so will your cook time—the average cook time is usually about 40 minutes).
4. When the potatoes are getting very close to being tender, warm the Cheesy Sauce and the beans in separate pans.
5. To assemble: Plate the potatoes and cut them across the top. Then, pry them open with a fork—just enough to get all the goodies in there. Top each potato with the Cheesy Sauce, beans, tomatoes, scallions, cilantro and jalapeño, and avocado if using. Enjoy immediately.

Nutrition:

- Calories: 420
- Total Fat: 5g
- Saturated Fat: 0g
- Cholesterol: 0mg
- Sodium: 503mg
- Carbohydrates: 80g
- Fiber: 17g
- Protein: 15g

Sausage, Ham and Hash Brown Bake

Preparation Time: 45 minutes

Cooking Time: 30 minutes

Servings: 4

Ingredients:

- ½ Pound chicken sausages, smoked
- ½ pound ham, sliced
- 6 oz. Hash browns, frozen and shredded
- 2 garlic cloves, minced
- 8 oz. Spinach
- ½ cup ricotta cheese
- ½ cup asiago cheese, grated
- 4 eggs
- ½ cup yogurt
- ½ cup milk
- Salt and ground black pepper, to taste
- 1 tsp. Smoked paprika

Directions:

1. Start by preheating your Air Fryer to 380°F. Cook the sausages and ham for 10 minutes; set them aside.
2. Meanwhile, in a preheated saucepan, cook the hash browns and garlic for 4 minutes, stirring frequently;

remove from the heat, add the spinach, and cover with the lid.

3. Allow the spinach to wilt completely. Transfer the sautéed mixture to a baking pan. Add the reserved sausage and ham.

4. In a mixing dish, thoroughly combine the cheese, eggs, yogurt, milk, salt, pepper, and paprika. Pour the cheese mixture over the hash browns in the pan.

5. Place the baking pan in the cooking basket and cook for approximately 30 minutes or until everything is thoroughly cooked. Bon appétit!

Nutrition:

- Calories: 509
- Fat: 20.1g
- Carbs: 40g
- Protein41.2g:
- Sugar: 3.9g

Kids' Taquitos

Preparation Time: 5 minutes

Cooking Time: 7 minutes

Servings: 4

Ingredients:

- 8 corn tortillas
- Cooking oil spray (coconut, sunflower, or safflower)
- 1 (15-oz.) Can vegan refried beans
- 1 cup shredded vegan cheese
- Guacamole (optional)
- Cheesy sauce (optional)
- Vegan sour cream (optional)
- Fresh salsa (optional)

Directions:

1. Warm the tortillas (so they don't break): Run them underwater for a second and then place them in an oil-sprayed air fryer basket (stacking them is fine). Fry for 1 minute.
2. Remove to a flat surface, laying them out individually. Place an equal amount of the beans in a line down the center of each tortilla. Top with vegan cheese.
3. Roll the tortilla sides up over the filling and place them seam-side down in the air fryer basket (this will help them

seal so the tortillas don't fly open). Add just enough to fill the basket without them touching too much (you may need to do another batch, depending on the size of your air fryer basket).

4. Spray the tops with oil. Fry for 7 minutes, or until the tortillas are golden brown and lightly crisp. Serve immediately with your preferred toppings.

Nutrition:

- Calories: 286
- Total Fat: 9g
- Saturated Fat: 4g
- Cholesterol: 0mg
- Sodium: 609mg
- Carbohydrates: 44g
- Fiber: 9g
- Protein: 9g

Immune-Boosting Grilled Cheese Sandwich

Preparation Time: 3 minutes

Cooking Time: 12 minutes

Servings: 1

Ingredients:

- 2 slices sprouted whole-grain bread (or substitute a gluten-free bread)
- 1 tsp. Vegan margarine or neutral-flavored oil (sunflower, safflower, or refined coconut)
- 2 slices vegan cheese (violife cheddar or Chao creamy original) or cheesy sauce
- 1 tsp. Mellow white miso
- 1 medium-large garlic clove, pressed or finely minced
- 2 tbsps. Fermented vegetables, kimchi, or sauerkraut
- Romaine or green leaf lettuce

Directions:

1. Spread the outsides of the bread with vegan margarine. Place the sliced cheese inside and close the sandwich back up again (buttered sides facing out). Place the sandwich in the air fryer basket and fry for 6 minutes. Flip over and fry for another 6 minutes, or until nicely browned and crisp on the outside.

2. Transfer to a plate. Open the sandwich and evenly spread the miso and garlic clove over the inside of 1 of the bread slices. Top with the fermented vegetables and lettuce, close the sandwich back up, cut in half, and serve it immediately.

Nutrition:

- Calories: 288
- Total Fat: 13g
- Saturated Fat: 5g
- Cholesterol: 0mg
- Sodium: 1013mg
- Carbohydrates: 34g
- Fiber: 4g
- Protein: 8g

Tamale Pie with Cilantro Lime Cornmeal Crust

Preparation Time: 25 minutes

Cooking Time: 20 minutes

Servings: 4

Ingredients:

For The Filling:

- 1 medium zucchini, diced (1¼ cups)
- 2 tsps. neutral-flavored oil (sunflower, safflower, or refined coconut)
- 1 cup cooked pinto beans, drained
- 1 cup canned diced tomatoes (unsalted) with juice
- 3 large garlic cloves, minced or pressed
- 1 tbsp. chickpea flour
- 1 tsp. dried oregano
- 1 tsp. onion granules
- ½ tsp. salt
- ½ tsp. crushed red chili flakes
- Cooking oil spray (sunflower, safflower, or refined coconut)

For The Crust:

- ½ cup yellow cornmeal, finely ground
- 1½ cups water

- ½ tsp. salt
- 1 tsp. Nutrition yeast
- 1 tsp. neutral-flavored oil (sunflower, safflower, or refined coconut)
- 2 tbsps. finely chopped cilantro
- ½ tsp. lime zest (see Cooking Tip)

Directions:

To Make the Filling:

1. In a large skillet set to medium-high heat, sauté the zucchini and oil for 3 minutes, or until the zucchini begins to brown.
2. Add the beans, tomatoes, garlic, flour, oregano, onion, salt, and chili flakes to the mixture. Cook over medium heat, stirring often, for 5 minutes, or until the mixture is thickened and no liquid remains. Remove from the heat.
3. Spray a 6-inch round, 2-inch-deep baking pan with oil and place the mixture in the bottom. Smooth out the top and set it aside.

To Make the Crust:

1. In a medium pot over high heat, place the cornmeal, water, and salt. Whisk constantly as you bring the mixture to a boil. Once it boils, reduce the heat to very low. Add the nutritional yeast and oil and continue to cook, stirring very often, for 10 minutes or until the mixture is very thick and hard to whisk. Remove from the heat.

2. Stir the cilantro and lime zest into the cornmeal mixture until thoroughly combined. Using a rubber spatula, gently spread it evenly onto the filling in the baking pan to form a smooth crust topping. Place in the air fryer basket and bake for 20 minutes, or until the top is golden brown. Let it cool for 5 to 10 minutes, then cut and serve it.

Nutrition:

- Calories: 165
- Total Fat: 5g
- Saturated Fat: 1g
- Cholesterol: 0mg
- Sodium: 831mg
- Carbohydrates: 26g
- Fiber: 6g
- Protein: 6g

Air Fryer Chicken Wings

Preparation Time: 5 minutes

Cooking Time: 20 minutes

Servings: 4

Ingredients:

- 4 (4-oz.) chicken wings
- 2 cloves garlic, finely minced
- Sea salt
- Freshly ground black pepper
- Smoked paprika
- Onion powder
- Olive oil

Directions:

1. Take the chicken wing parts out of the refrigerator and pat them dry (if you remove as much moisture as possible, you will get a crispy wing skin).
2. Mix sea salt, black pepper, smoked paprika, garlic powder, onion powder, and baking powder in a small bowl or baking dish.
3. Sprinkle the spice mixture on the wings and throw it to cover.
4. Place the wings on the cooking basket. In the Ninja Foodie, this is known as the "Cook and Crisp" basket.

5. Drizzle the chicken wings with olive oil.
6. Use the Air Crisp setting at 400°F on air fryers to cook the wings for 14 minutes on each side.
7. Enjoy hot wings!

Nutrition:

- Calories: 32 kcal
- Protein: 2g
- Fat: 1.73g
- Carbohydrates: 2.56g

Buffalo Cauliflower Bites

Preparation Time: 5 minutes

Cooking Time: 25 minutes

Servings: 4

Ingredients:

- 3 tbsp. Extra-virgin olive oil, divided
- Kosher salt
- Cauliflower
- Garlic cloves
- Hot sauce
- Butter
- Worcestershire sauce
- Blue cheese

Directions:

1. Cut the cauliflower into florets of equal size and place it in a large bowl.
2. Cut each clove of garlic into 3 pieces and smash them with the side of your knife. Don't be afraid to smash the garlic. You want to expose as much of the garlic surface as possible so that it cooks well. Add this to the cauliflower.
3. Pour over the oil and add salt. Mix well until the cauliflower is well covered with oil and salt.

4. Turn on the air fryer at 400°F for 20 minutes and add the cauliflower. Turn it in half once.

To Make the Sauce:

1. While the cauliflower is cooking, make the sauce. Whisk the hot sauce, butter, and Worcestershire sauce in a small bowl.
2. Once the cauliflower is cooked, place it in a large bowl. Pour the hot sauce over the cauliflower and mix well.
3. Put the cauliflower back in the air fryer. Set it to 400°F for 3-4 minutes so the sauce becomes a little firm.
4. Serve with blue cheese dressing.

Nutrition:

- Calories: 69 kcal
- Protein: 1.87g
- Fat: 6.06g
- Carbohydrates: 1.99g

Chapter 5: Snack Recipes

Air Fryer Asparagus

Preparation Time: 5 minutes

Cooking Time: 8 minutes

Servings: 1

Ingredients:

- Nutritional yeast (1 condiment)
- Olive oil non-stick spray (1 healthy fat)
- 1 bunch of asparagus (9 greens)

Directions:

1. Wash the asparagus and do not forget to trim off the thick woody ends.
2. Spray the asparagus with olive oil spray and sprinkle with the yeast.
3. In your Instant Crisp Air Fryer, lay the asparagus in a singular layer. Set the temperature to 360°F. While the time limit to 8 minutes.

Nutrition:

- Calories 17:
- Fat: 4g
- Protein: 9g

Avocado Fries

Preparation Time: 10 minutes

Cooking Time: 7 minutes

Servings: 1

Ingredients:

- 1 avocado (2 healthy fats)
- 1/8 tsp. salt (¼ condiments)
- ¼ cup panko breadcrumbs (½ healthy fat)
- Bean liquid (aquafaba) a 15-oz. can of white or garbanzo beans (6 greens)

Directions:

1. Peel, pit, and slice up the avocado.
2. Toss salt and breadcrumbs together in a bowl. Place the aquafaba into another bowl.
3. Dredge slices of avocado first in the aquafaba and then in the panko, making sure you can coat them evenly.
4. Place the coated avocado slices into a single layer in the Instant Crisp Air Fryer. Set the temperature to 390°F and set the time to 5 minutes.
5. Serve it with your favorite Keto dipping sauce!

Nutrition:

- Calories: 102
- Protein: 9g

Bell-Pepper Wrapped in Tortilla

Preparation Time: 5 minutes

Cooking Time: 15 minutes

Servings: 1

Ingredients:

- ¼ Small red bell pepper (½ greens)
- ¼ tbsp. water (½ condiment)
- 1 large tortilla (1 healthy fat)
- 1 commercial vegan nuggets, chopped (3 leans)
- Mixed greens for garnish (6 greens)

Directions:

1. Preheat the Instant Crisp Air Fryer to 400°F.
2. In a skillet heated over medium heat, water sautés the vegan nuggets and bell peppers. Set them aside.
3. Place the filling inside the corn tortillas.
4. Fold the tortillas, place them inside the Instant Crisp Air Fryer and cook for 15 minutes until the tortilla wraps are crispy.
5. Serve with mixed greens on top.

Nutrition:

- Calories: 548
- Fat: 21g
- Protein: 46g

Crispy Roasted Broccoli

Preparation Time: 10 minutes

Cooking Time: 8 minutes

Servings: 1

Ingredients:

- ¼ tsp. Masala (½ condiment)
- ½ tsp. Red chili powder (1 condiment)
- ½ tsp. Salt (1 condiment)
- ¼ tsp. Turmeric powder (½ condiment)
- 1 tbsp. Chickpea flour (1 healthy fat)
- 1 tbsp. Yogurt (2 healthy fats)
- ½ pound broccoli (1 green)

Directions:

1. Cut the broccoli up into florets. Immerse in a bowl of water with 2 tsps. of salt for at least half an hour to remove impurities.
2. Take out the broccoli florets from the water and let them drain. Wipe them down thoroughly.
3. Mix all the other ingredients to create a marinade.
4. Toss the broccoli florets in the marinade. Cover and chill for 15-30 minutes.
5. Preheat the Instant Crisp Air Fryer to 390°F. Place the marinated broccoli florets into the fryer, lock the air fryer

lid, set the temperature to 350°F, and set the time to 10 minutes. Florets will be crispy when done.

Nutrition:

- Calories: 96
- Fat: 1.3g
- Protein: 7g

Coconut Battered Cauliflower Bites

Difficulty: Average

Preparation Time: 5 minutes

Cooking Time: 20 minutes

Servings: 1

Ingredients:

- Salt and pepper to taste (2 condiments)
- 1 flax egg or 1 tbsp. flaxseed meal + 3 tbsps. water (1 healthy fat)
- 1 small cauliflower, cut into florets (2 greens)
- 1 tsp. mixed spice (1 condiment)
- ½ tsp. mustard powder (1 condiment)
- 2 tbsps. maple syrup (2 healthy fats)
- 1 clove of garlic, minced (1 green)
- 2 tbsps. soy sauce (2 condiments)
- 1/3 cup oats flour (½ healthy fat)
- 1/3 cup plain flour (½ healthy fat)
- 1/3 cup desiccated coconut (½ lean)

Directions:

1. In a mixing bowl, mix the oats, flour, and desiccated coconut. Season with salt and pepper to taste. Set them aside.

2. In another bowl, place the flax egg and add a pinch of salt to taste. Set them aside.

3. Season the cauliflower with mixed spice and mustard powder.

4. Dredge the florets in the flax egg first, then in the flour mixture.

5. Place inside the Instant Crisp Air Fryer, lock the air fryer lid, and cook at 400°F for 15 minutes.

6. Meanwhile, place the maple syrup, garlic, and soy sauce in a saucepan and heat over medium flame. Wait for it to boil and adjust the heat to low until the sauce thickens.

7. After 15 minutes, take out the Instant Crisp Air Fryer's florets and place them in the saucepan.

8. Toss to coat the florets and place inside the Instant Crisp Air Fryer and cook them for another 5 minutes.

Nutrition:

- Calories: 154
- Fat: 2.3g
- Protein: 4.6g

Crispy Jalapeno Coins

Preparation Time: 10 minutes

Cooking Time: 5 minutes

Servings: 1

Ingredients:

- 1 egg (1 healthy fat)
- 2-3 tbsp. Coconut flour (1 healthy fat)
- 1 sliced and seeded jalapeno (2 greens)
- Pinch of garlic powder (1 condiment)
- Bit of Cajun seasoning (optional)
- Pinch of pepper and salt (1 condiment)

Directions:

1. Prepare the ingredients. Ensure your Instant Crisp Air Fryer is preheated to 400°F.
2. Mix all the dry ingredients.
3. Pat the jalapeno slices dry. Dip coins into the egg wash and then into the dry mixture. Toss to coat thoroughly.
4. Add the coated jalapeno slices to the Instant Crisp Air Fryer in a single layer. Spray with olive oil.
5. Lock the air fryer lid. Set the temperature to 350°F and set the time to 5 minutes. Cook just till crispy.

Nutrition:

- Calories: 128

- Fat: 8g
- Protein: 7g

Slow Cooker Savory Butternut Squash Oatmeal

Preparation Time: 15 minutes

Cooking Time: 6 to 8 hours

Servings: 1

Ingredients:

- ¼ cup steel-cut oats (½ healthy fat)
- ½ cups cubed (½-inch pieces) peeled butternut squash (1 green)
- ¾ cups of water (1 healthy fat)
- 1/16 cup unsweetened nondairy milk (1/8 healthy fat)
- ¼ tbsp. Chia seed (½ healthy fat)
- ½ tsp. Yellow (mellow) miso paste (1 condiment)
- ¾ tsp. Ground ginger (1 condiment)
- ¼ tbsp. Sesame seed, toasted (½ healthy fat)
- ¼ tbsp. Chopped scallion, green parts only (1 green)
- Shredded carrot, for serving (optional) (1 green)

Directions:

1. In a slow cooker, combine the oats, butternut squash, and water.
2. Cover the slow cooker and cook on low for 6 to 8 hours or until the squash is fork-tender. Using a potato masher or

heavy spoon, roughly mash the cooked butternut squash. Stir to combine with the oats.

3. Whisk together the milk, chia seeds, miso paste, and ginger to combine in a large bowl. Stir the mixture into the oats.

4. Top your oatmeal bowl with sesame seeds and scallion for more plant-based fiber, top with shredded carrot (if using).

Nutrition:

- Calories: 230
- Fat: 5g
- Protein: 7g

Carrot Cake Oatmeal

Preparation Time: 10 minutes

Cooking Time: 15 minutes

Servings: 1

Ingredients:

- 1/8 cup pecans (¼ healthy fat)
- ½ cup finely shredded carrot (1 green)
- ¼ cup old-fashioned oats (½ healthy fat)
- 5/8 cups unsweetened non-dairy milk (¼ healthy fat)
- ½ tablespoon pure maple syrup (1 healthy fat)
- ½ tsp. Ground cinnamon (1 condiment)
- ½ tsp. Ground ginger (1 condiment)
- 1/8 tsp. Ground nutmeg (¼ condiment)
- 1 tbsp. Chia seed (1 healthy fat)

Directions:

1. Over medium-high heat in a skillet, toast the pecans for 3 to 4 minutes, often stirring, until browned and fragrant (watch closely, as they can burn quickly). Pour the pecans onto a cutting board and coarsely chop them. Set them aside.

2. Using an 8-quart pot at medium-high heat, combine the carrot, oats, milk, maple syrup, cinnamon, ginger, and nutmeg. When it is already boiling, reduce the heat to

medium-low. Cook, uncovered, for 10 minutes, stirring occasionally.

3. Stir in the chopped pecans and chia seeds. Serve them immediately.

Nutrition:

- Calories: 307
- Fat: 17g
- Protein: 7g

Spiced Sorghum and Berries

Preparation Time: 5 minutes

Cooking Time: 1 hour

Servings: 1

Ingredients:

- ¼ cup whole-grain sorghum (½ healthy fat)
- ¼ tsp. Ground cinnamon (½ condiment)
- ¼ tsp. Chinese 5-spice powder (½ condiment)
- ¾ cups water (1 condiment)
- ¼ cup nondairy milk, unsweetened (½ healthy fat)
- ¼ tsp. Vanilla extract (½ healthy fat)
- ½ tablespoons pure maple syrup (1 healthy fat)
- ½ tablespoon chia seed (1 healthy fat)
- 1/8 cup sliced almonds (¼ lean)
- ½ cups fresh raspberries, divided (1 lean)

Directions:

1. Using a large pot over medium-high heat, stir together the sorghum, cinnamon, 5-spice powder, and water. Wait for the water to boil, cover it and reduce the heat to medium-low. Cook for 1 hour, or until the sorghum is soft and chewy. If the sorghum grains are still hard, add another cup of water and cook for 15 minutes more.

2. Using a glass measuring cup, whisk together the milk, vanilla, and maple syrup to blend. Add the mixture to the sorghum and the chia seeds, almonds, and 1 cup of raspberries. Gently stir to combine.

3. When serving, top with the remaining 1 cup of fresh raspberries.

Nutrition:

- Calories: 289
- Fat: 8g
- Protein: 9g

Spiced Pumpkin Muffins

Preparation Time: 15 minutes

Cooking Time: 20 minutes

Servings: 1

Ingredients:

- 1/6 tbsp. Ground flaxseed (¼ healthy fat)
- 1/24 cup water (¼ condiment)
- 1/8 cups whole wheat flour (¼ healthy fat)
- 1/6 tsp. Baking powder (1/3 healthy fat)
- 5/6 tsp. Ground cinnamon (¼ condiment)
- 1/12 tsp. Baking soda (1/8 condiment)
- 1/12 tsp. Ground ginger (1/8 condiment)
- 1/16 tsp. Ground nutmeg (1/8 condiment)
- 1/32 tsp. Ground cloves (1/8 condiment)
- 1/6 cup pumpkin puree (1/3 healthy fat)
- 1/12 cup pure maple syrup (1/8 healthy fat)
- 1/24 cup unsweetened applesauce (1/8 healthy fat)
- 1/24 cup unsweetened nondairy milk (1/8 healthy fat)
- ½ tsp. Vanilla extract (1 healthy fat)

Directions:

1. Preheat the oven to 350°F. Line a 12-cup metal muffin pan with parchment paper liners or use a silicone muffin pan.

2. First, mix the flaxseed and water in a large bowl and then keep it aside.
3. In a medium bowl, stir together the flour, baking powder, cinnamon, baking soda, ginger, nutmeg, and cloves.
4. In a medium bowl, stir up the maple syrup, pumpkin puree, applesauce, milk, and vanilla. Using a spatula, mix the wet ingredients with the dry ones.
5. Fold the soaked flaxseed into the batter until evenly combined, but do not overmix the batter, or your muffins will become dense. Ladle the batter with a ½ cup per muffin into your prepared muffin pan.
6. Bake for 18 to 20 minutes. Remove the muffins from the pan.
7. Transfer them to a wire rack for cooling.
8. Store them in an air-tight container at room temperature.

Nutrition:

- Calories: 115
- Fat: 1g
- Protein: 3g

Plant-Powered Pancakes

Preparation Time: 5 minutes

Cooking Time: 15 minutes

Servings: 8

Ingredients:

- 1 cup whole-wheat flour (1 healthy fat)
- 1 tsp. baking powder (½ healthy fat)
- ½ tsp. ground cinnamon (½ condiment)
- 1 cup plant-based milk (1 healthy fat)
- ½ cup unsweetened applesauce (1 healthy fat)
- ¼ cup maple syrup (½ healthy fat)
- 1 tsp. vanilla extract (1 healthy fat)

Directions:

1. In a large bowl, combine the flour, baking powder, and cinnamon.
2. Stir in the milk, applesauce, maple syrup, and vanilla until no dry flour is left and the batter is smooth.
3. Preheat a huge, non-stick skillet over medium heat. For each pancake, pour ¼ cup of batter onto the hot skillet. Once bubbles form over the top of the pancake and the sides begin to brown, flip and cook for 1 to 2 more minutes.
4. Repeat until all the batter is used and serve it.

Nutrition:

- Calories: 591
- Fat: 2g
- Protein: 5g

Sweet Cashew Cheese Spread

Preparation Time: 5 minutes

Cooking Time: 5 minutes

Servings: 10

Ingredients:

- Stevia (5 drops) (½ condiment)
- Cashews (2 cups, raw) (3 healthy fats)
- Water (½ cup) (1 condiment)

Directions:

1. Soak the cashews overnight in water.
2. Next, drain the excess water, then transfer the cashews to a food processor.
3. Add in the stevia and the water.
4. Process until smooth.
5. Serve it chilled. Enjoy.

Nutrition:

- Calories: 322
- Fat: 7g
- Protein: 5.7g

Mini Zucchini Bites

Preparation Time: 10 minutes

Cooking Time: 10 minutes

Servings: 6

Ingredients:

- 1 zucchini, cut into thick circles (2 greens)
- 3 cherry tomatoes, halved (6 greens)
- ½ cup parmesan cheese, grated (1 healthy fat)
- Salt and pepper to taste (1 condiment)
- 1 tsp. Chives, chopped (1 green)

Directions:

1. Preheat the oven to 390°F.
2. Add wax paper to a baking sheet.
3. Arrange the zucchini pieces.
4. Add the cherry halves to each zucchini slice.
5. Add parmesan cheese, chives and sprinkle with salt and pepper.
6. Bake for 10 minutes. Serve it.

Nutrition:

- Calories: 361
- Fat: 1g
- Protein: 7.3g

Crispy Cauliflowers

Preparation Time: 10 minutes

Cooking Time: 10 minutes

Servings: 4

Ingredients:

- 2 cup cauliflower florets, diced (6 greens)
- ½ cup almond flour (1 healthy fat)
- ½ cup coconut flour (1 healthy fat)
- Salt and pepper to taste (½ condiment)
- 1 tsp. Mixed herbs (1 green)
- 1 tsp. Chives, chopped (1 green)
- 1 egg (1 lean)
- 1 tsp. Cumin (1 condiment)
- ½ tsp. Garlic powder (1 condiment)
- 1 cup water (1 condiment)
- Oil for frying (1 condiment)

Directions:

1. Combine the egg, salt, garlic, water, cumin, chives, mixed herbs, pepper, and flour in a mixing bowl.
2. Stir in the cauliflower to the mixture and then fry them in oil until they become golden in color.
3. Serve it.

Nutrition:

- Calories: 259
- Protein: 3.3g
- Fat: 10.4g

CPSIA information can be obtained
at www.ICGtesting.com
Printed in the USA
LVHW080824200721
693060LV00007B/51